C000111922

A Bin Night in November

NATURE POEMS VOLUME 1

Black Cat Poetry Press

Editor: Satya Bosman
Artist Design: Lucia Bosman
www.blackcatpress.co.uk

Copyright © 2022

All rights reserved. No part of this book may be reproduced in
any manner whatsoever without written permission of the
authors except in the case of reprints in the context of reviews.

Cover art design by Lucia Bosman
ISBN: 978-1-7397811-0-1

'...and then, I have nature and art and poetry, and if that is not enough, what is enough?'

Vincent van Gogh

Editorial Note

Welcome to our debut anthology at Black Cat Press, *A Bin Night in November,* named after one of the poems included in this book by Lisa Simpson. Whenever I see the moon on a clear crisp evening, I think of this poem.

In *River* by Victoria Punch, she talks about how the river makes the rain beautiful, such an elegant way to describe the connectedness of nature. Daniel Moreschi's *Demise of the Bees* warns of 'human hubris makes a baneful way', a caution that we are close to the plight of the honeybee and not to let our hubris lead to our mutual end.

In *Little Boats* by Bronwen R. C. Evans, the blossoms tease us to go with them on their travels before they 'pirouette and gently sit'. It makes me think that so much of who we are as people imitate the forms and movement we find in nature.

I'll never be able to plant vegetables in my garden again without thinking of 'lips like bitter-lemon purses' in Barry Hollow's *Vegetable Gardening with Jessie is a prickly business,* it is such an evocative description I can't help but pinch my lips when I read it.

Corinna Board's poem *'The stripped tree boughs comfort me drawn clear against the sky'* After Margaret Widdemer, says *'We are not unalike, I think'* which gives us permission to befriend and even love this tree whose circumstances might mirror our own at times.

Richard S. Parrett invites us in *Walk with Me* to '…steps which weave white cliffs, and buckle on forest floors'. If ever I want to amble through nature in my mind, I read this poem. It tells us we are but passing through and that nature greets every generation the same, another important reason to preserve its majesty for future generations.

This book is an ode to nature and hopefully a place to retreat to during difficult times. To remind us of what we have and what we must protect.

As Samuel Mackereth says so beautifully in *By the Island Pool* 'my brief foray will barely scratch the skin of its rich body, let alone the heart'.

This is the first book to preserve in print some of the poets we admire and love to read.

Thank you to all the poets for their bountiful, imagistic, and lyrical poems. A portion of the profits of this publication will go to preserving trees and planting new trees.

We hope you enjoy this book.

Best,

Satya Bosman
Editor, Black Cat Poetry Press

Contents

A Bin Night in November

I tread carefully on these steps,
where slick green moss is felted to the damp stone.
The door behind me closes and the warm light of home
dissolves in the darkness.
Winter has blown in and
the bitter air bites through to bone.

Tangled high in the silhouette of the sleeping tree,
the moon is full and white
and she glows and she flickers
as bare branches sway, softly.
Frost sparkles and wisps of warm breath dance.
The night is as clear as glass.

And it is quiet. And it is still.

I pause, black bag in hand,
as the rest of the world folds itself away.
It is just me right now, alone,
beneath the milk moon,
a smattering of stars
and a sky of spilled ink blue.

Lisa Simpson

An Ode to Autumn

Soft orange flesh scooped out and spiced,
warm comfort rises from the pot on the stove
and steams up cold black windows.
In the doorstep's shadow, a gentle light flickers
within the empty remains of the plump orange fruit.
The quiet air is damp, thick with cold wisps of burnt smoke,
from the first-lit log fires of the season, or
the exhalation of a thousand sky-fallen fireworks.
Tomorrow we will walk beneath boughs ablaze,
crackling underfoot, scarlet and syrup gold in the lazy morning sun.
Autumn is an orange flame.

Lisa Simpson

Morning Song

Beneath the shade of the sycamore tree,
where soft velvet moss
mottles the threadbare lawn,
I sit with you.
The carpet of spotted dead-nettle
hums gently, silvery leaves ripple
on the breath of a spring breeze.
Threads of gold weave through rustling boughs
as the sun sears her path above the rooftops.
Birdsong tinkling. Dawn's dewy scent.
Somewhere, the clattering of crockery as
the rest of the world rises from slumber.
Solitude, cornflower skies and cool air soothes.
I realise
you are gone.

Lisa Simpson

Odyssey of the Hine's Emerald Dragonfly

A mother roams nemoral bounds, where roots and rims embrace
A sunken ark, that fends barrage, as scattered ripples chase.
A rustling span descends as emeralds, enlivened, tell
Of a turning dragon's tail within a leafy citadel.

From dormant lay, a dawn from gloom, while famished pores collect;
A flurry flings a flap, and falling cradle feigns neglect,
And breaches bed of swaddling swing, that brings abyssal brink:
The nascence of a nymph amid the liquid lanes to slink.

Along a luminous roulette of rooted frays surveyed,
A small amalgam gathers as an aqua masquerade.
Though raids from show of sprightly strides reveal a vital script,
That leads to carcasses as spoils, to yield a stratum stripped.

From growth a flow, through chancy streams, while spurred by flanks asprout,
Prevailing gulfs of gills and guillotines, with rise or rout.
A final shed at shallow depths, and then a brisk ascent
Of paper pillars on compelling urge to reinvent.

On brace of motes, a break from mould, as quaking seams unearth
A base of beats, awaiting wands of wander from rebirth.
While coated peak emboldens leaps, when lustrous yarn combines,
To render flight from cling that leaves behind the leaves as Hine's.

Daniel Moreschi

Demise of the Bees

Where golden glare enkindles blossoms, gowned
By jewelled grains encased in layers wound,
A wooden palace would befit a queen
Of black and yellow subjects, once abound.

With floaty whims and homing hums between
The swaying filaments from their routine
As architects of bloom, till sparse array
Is pressing cause to mourn patrols unseen.

The placid soils and glades become a fray
On sight of steel jaws and a scything sway,
As all the rooted flee their havens old
When human hubris makes a baneful way.

In hives as naves come heists for liquid gold,
While through the fields are crops as altars tolled
With poison chalices, to purge the meek,
Despite the harvest scripts that they uphold.

And from ceaseless emissions of carbon cauldron peak
Are swarms immersed, as stirred horizons wreak,
While hasty cycles render sprouting sown
And seeds to perish as a stranded streak.

With ends of lines as trigger to bemoan
The tilt of timeless balance to atone,
When nature's feeding chains of prey are thrown
And terra parched is course of downfall shown.

Daniel Moreschi

The Moth

Above a woody balcony, a shade
Stirs and displays a speckled wings' cascade,
And seeks relief within the grasp of night,
When routes are guided by beguiling light.

Beyond the trees, a binding loop along
A lush expanse, where lunar seams prolong
A wish to synchronise at blissful peaks,
And trace the trails of asterismal streaks.

While clouds are fractured, they allow a trend
Of stellar pirouettes, before a leaden blend
Envelops, as the moon begins to blink,
And lifts revert to flits around the brink.

From dark periphery, the forlorn loom
Pursues reflections by a weeping bloom.
Its restlessness, a yonder twinkle baits,
And beckons, where a bolted beacon waits.

On reach to warmth that welcomes coalesce,
A giddy glide writhes from faux egress
Where beams appear to pledge a union yearned,
Yet leave an aftermath of remnants burned.

Daniel Moreschi

Blue Sky

like an oil painter's board
pure. primary.
under the blooming cloud - thick
palette knife spread
the sun fell into the field
and burst into bright laughter
burning on the field
- oilseed yellow
bottle and bake these golden moments for
the year rolls on
the clock clicks
the soil turns over
and abed we find the winter
brown and grey
and wait

Victoria Punch

Morning Light

I am a collection of morning
following blue into the eye
of the rock.
Steady ground, soft ocean
underlit cloud over the waterlap
creeping coral and kelp from the dark
of the night sea
hush with the day
let the soft wind carry;
all things change but the
rock, anchored by the tide to the seabed,
mirrored in the light of the morning

Victoria Punch

River~

flowing down the landscape
bends and turns, you twine
twistvined, longlined you
change the shape of where we are
lilac layers and white wavelets
in the wind – you – feathered
side-by-side by green
against the sky your purple depths
and petalled drops and
drapes you hang, you fall
you take the rain and make it
beautiful

~Wisteria

Victoria Punch

By the Island Pool

The Earth tugs at my sleeve, child-like, these days
and forces me to stop and notice things—
the flight of crows that wheel above the oak,
the way my breath hangs longer every minute in the air
that cools and sinks from Axborough Wood to cloak
the Island Pool.
I think the sky is flirting with the bracken,
matching the burning bronze with a diffusing blush
of soft, ethereal rose.

'Enough', She says, 'look closer for the cut
of an individual wing and how it carves the air
in a bright arc from earth to heaven and back just for the joy
of being there. Breathe in the musk of leaves descending into
Winter's sleep;
pick out the pearly Amanitas— bracken covered,
cloaking their fatal secret.
Listen beyond the stillness for the ducks
that settle on the water
and the horses
bidding the fields goodnight for heat and hay.
Stay
out a little while and watch the rose
melt into shadow, splinter into stars.
Each is a promise: beauty exists, eternal,
beyond our little lives yet we
are just divine enough to taste
this minute fraction of its dizzy draught.'

I am finding, out here, that I know next to nothing
of the unfathomable vast of all that is.
My brief foray will barely scratch the skin
of its rich body, let alone the heart.
I am learning that existence is motion, everything
is coming from one place or state of being and moves
or shifts into another.
Our place, if any, in life's tumbling stream
is to find stillness in the eddies and admire
the flight of things around us, and our own.

Samuel Mackereth

Desdemona

I see her through screens of bright alder;
Sun-kissed catkins and leaves too green,
Too innocent to weather Winter.
The memory is a dance, dysfluent;
A divided duty;
A war of pain and pleasure,
Heat and cold.

Her roots dig in my mind and planted there
She'll never rot or perish, rather grow
And stretch her soft-boned fingers out like vines
Frost-blanched, silk-skinned
Through time
To vice my heart.

In memory she is crowned
With bright-white roses and their thorns,
A flawless Desdemona diadem
In silver light drawn heavy on her brow.
She drifts to me in dreams on floating feet but
Inches, eggshell steps, above black water—but
An inch beneath my skin.

And still in sleep she chides me—reproachful Nightingale!
Upon my shoulder, around my neck, relentless—
Incessant dripping of these rainy days...
That my unkindness did defeat her life
That night, that I might live today—
Oh, bitter fruit of sweetest flower was this
Most undeserved farewell!

Samuel Mackereth

Snow on the White Peak

The snow snuck in last night at 3am; I woke
And Matlock Moor was bright with it. The conifers
Stood heavy with the weight of ice
And trembled in its grip. I thought
The golden light of morning might
Dissolve its onslaught, as the night
Gave way to glorious day. The gale
Pursued it though, the furious gale
That chased it here. The gale was not
Content to let the white flakes rest
But ripped them up from their fresh bed
And whipped them up into a head to scour
Like sand each hill and dale and test
The mettle of the unsuspecting land in a white war.

I trod the path up Wetton Hill today, to see
If snow and wind and cold could conquer me.
I felt its angry eddies lash my face,
I stumbled like a drunkard in its drifts,
I gave my bones up to its deepest chills
And felt its bright perfection blur my sight;
But all I found was stillness in the storm, stillness
Beyond the sheep that shelter by the wall, beyond
The gate (half buried) and the trees (leafless,
Ice-barked) that mark the village bound. I looked
Beyond the howl and saw a world, frozen
Mid-flow: cars stuck, lights out, and peace: silence
Of bird and farm and car and radio—
Silence beyond the gale, beneath the snow.

Samuel Mackereth

I Find You in the Forest

Today you were the squirrels
carrying the conkers by mouth
that we would hang from string,
no games just aurum fur
crossing my path
moon bellied, starlit eyes
collecting clues, carefully
creating your almanac
so cosy midnights are
no little creature's mere dream,
joyful towards the undergrowth.

Bronwen R. C. Evans

Golden Fields

If I had a dark vault
filled with riches
I would lighten it
and build tiny fences
behind all the roadside bushes,
insects come and go
as they please
birds settle easily on leaves
and little four legs
are kept safe
in the green, no gentle
tragic tarmac corpses
to be seen.

Bronwen R.C. Evans

Little Boats

Past my window sailing petals
teaching us the way the wind blows
summer snow it does not stop,
we see little else
and follow the travel of this waltz
across ever-forming stacked horizons.

Gently flowing tender bricks,
the real world behind; cement in between.
Drawing light from sunshine beams
catching tides like racing ships
until the last blossom falls alone,
pirouettes and gently sits.

Bronwen R.C. Evans

My Queen (a palindrome poem)

more than a Monarch
Butterflies
she dances
over wild poppy fields,
entrances, flitting as she feels
at ease on rhythmic summer breeze,
she dances,
to tease her music
from West Coast seas,
frees a siren's serenade.
Enticing to drop from edges
of horizon
dropping dark honey,
golden drips slip
into my thunder-struck heart.
a maelstrom of a Kelpie spirit,
she dances

My Queen

Barry Hollow

Lumbert wi boonty (original Scots)

Kinlt lugs and glowerin twigs
warm weary shin.
Banes baukit in yit anither windae.
Neu barn hame coories in
wi rustic saunstane wa's
an tidy thatch abin heids.
Tups, dugs, hoolets an hawks,
scraich aroon dreich mossbanks
ae braw reservoir-amphitheatre nichts.
The panoply ae fauna
perfectly wheeshtin acroass the panorama
as een pan across, nae dramas.
Mindfu'ness spills ivver
tae fill ma widden quaich
fir company's a laden plate.
Haufwey up the gully,
ganderin doon on geese
whae skip watter lik smooth slate stanes
stealth mode ghostin,
ant-motor ermy troops trope,
wheech bye oan horizon,
lumbert wi boonty

Barry Hollow

Lumbered with bounty
(English translation)

Kindled logs and glowering twigs
warm weary feet.
Bones comfy in yet another window.
New barn home cuddles in
with rustic sandstone walls
and tidy thatch above heads.
Sheep, dogs, owls and hawks,
screech around drab mossbanks
of beautiful reservoir-amphitheatre nights.
The panoply of fauna
perfectly quieting across the panorama,
as eyes pan across, no dramas.
Mindfulness spills over
to fill ma wooden quaich
for company's a laden plate.
Halfway up the ravine,
gandering down on geese
who skip water like smooth slate stones,
stealth mode ghosting,
ant-motor army troops trope,
whizz past on horizon,
lumbered with bounty.

Barry Hollow

Vegetable Gardening With Jessie
Is a Prickly Business

Stood on the back step in Coronation Road,
three feet from an expanse
of precious raised beds.
All 20ft of the Guardian Monkey-Puzzle tree looming.
Staunch in her pilgrimage to horizon,
we shiver in the sun
and the shadow. Tentative hands cradle eggshells
from breakfast,
as if their heads aren't already caved in.
Now, ghosts haunt the mountain
of scotch pancakes who bulge our bellies.
Belies the forecast of a spectre
at my shoulder, with fistfuls of frigid tea bags.
Long, iron limbs and stoop of a willow.
I never question the teabag origin story,
although this soft Ice Queen drinks cool, boiled water.
I gather the caved-in eggshells heads
and tea bags, to scatter their shrapnel
as we'll spread her ashes.
The rockery, primed for fresh cactus juice,
tucked away at the back.
All crazy-paving, prickly sticks and fuzzy watermelons, all begging
to be tested for the gift of feeling (something).
You're never at my shoulder for this
as it's unapproved, stolen time, away from you.
Your lips are unapproving, bitter-lemon purses,
still surreptitiously, not staring
through the kitchen window.
Wringing cheesecloth and tracing paper knuckle skin.
You walked away.

Barry Hollow

A Matriarch

As the daylight hours narrow and night-time prevails
her branches with dropped leaves and bare limbs
lie fallow,

their latticework of fine twigs, some knotty
ending in cloying buds
branching from the bough.

Dusk breaks and a tawny owl resting on her limbs
listens patiently for the scurrying under a covering of snow,
to pounce!

A fox calls out, the sound carrying in the still winter air
as it tramples over the bearded tooth fungus, winter green ferns and
climbing feathery plumes at the base of her trunk.

Underground, her roots, wide spreading
growing in the old fallen leaves
bring sugar to her and her saplings.

Satya Bosman

A Winter's Child

I am a winter's child
the familiar frost
welcomes me into its quiet
as I amble. The holly poking through ice crystals,

each one a unique pattern
a lone robin on its branches
a fox leaving footprints in the snow.
An avenue of branches

shaped like bony fingers
that point to gardens
otherwise hidden by overgrown rusted gates.
Gardens with winter honeysuckle,

its cream-white flowers on leafless branches
and snowdrops starting to appear,
heralding the end of winter
and the long wait until

the next fresh fallen snow,
to cover your tracks

Satya Bosman

Seasons

The air filled with the smell of leaves,
fallen and unattended.
The sky white as bone.
The trees bare, lung shaped branches
waiting
to cast off the stillness of the day,
for threads of sunlight to grow
stronger and blow life into the corridor of veins
from bark to leaf.
To welcome strangers taking shelter in their shade
in drawn out afternoons, until the light softly fades.

Satya Bosman

'The stripped tree boughs comfort me drawn clear against the sky'
After Margaret Widdemer

I let my gaze wander over barren branches,
stark black against the winter sky.
We are not unalike, I think.
You, too, have suffered loss,
been stripped bare by the passage of time,
yet you welcome change with open arms;
gracefully clocking the seasons
with each new ring inside your trunk,
each beat of your sap-fuelled heart.
When the last leaves have fallen,
you do not grieve or look down,
instead you reach into the grey
and pull hope from the clouds –
tucking it under your bark,
holding it close.

Corinna Board

Counting Sheep

A golden shovel after Sheep in Fog by Sylvia Plath

The morning sky is bright blue, but my
heart is full of rain; it seeps into my bones;
ushered by November's cold winds. I hold
on to the feeling as the hours tick by, until a
sense of comfort emerges from the stillness
of the new day—how the earth slowly wakens to the
rhythmic lull of birdsong. I close my eyes: far
in the distance, I imagine the mist-veiled fields
quietly preparing for Winter; the icy months will melt
into Spring eventually, but first the days must shorten. My
thoughts turn to you—I gather your darkness & cradle it in my heart.

Corinna Board

How To Make It Through the Winter

This morning
I swallowed a slice of sky,
& my world turned from grey to blue:
the clouds in my heart have flown;
blown south by December's winds,
& even the rain tastes sweeter now.
My mind is a whirl of hungry birds,
the tired grass lies heavy on the ground,
but somewhere under all that mud,
spring hums like a swarm of bees:
biding her time, almost ready.

Corinna Board

Walk With Me

Walk with me on steps which weave
white cliffs, and buckle on forest floors
climb mountains to ascend, on high
laced clouds which lead to nowhere —
as I am to the crashing waves
just passing through

Walk with me through fields and heath
dry thistle and wheat, windswept
steep woods which step to pastures green
stone-walls which guide to open gates —
as I am to the flowing stream
just passing through

Walk with me along pebbled shores
from west to east, as starlings sway
thick moss laid moors that fade to grey
and shelter in caves which rise —
as I am to the rain on a summer's day
just passing through

Richard S. Parrett

Our Woodlands

Ancient crowns found in burial grounds
far from the Venus of our Woods
and the Queen of British Trees flowers
as we wander below auburn canopies
Aspen, Ash and Beech

The Elm drops its branches
in which we lay to rest our dead
as the gentle Hornbeam splays

In soft green light finches collect
their seeds, and the Oak offers fruits
while ruling with a bygone majesty

The Willow shakes in clement climes
as catkins drift downstream, and
lovers lay on beds of needles
by a woodland weaved with Yew

Richard S. Parrett

Bonsai

Our little Bonsai tree
with all your aches and pains
longing to be free
in the Kamakura rain

Austere in their practice
hachi-no-ki with intent
the Zen make time for ritual
with a mind never bent

In the West we prune and pinch
we borrow, beg and steal
a thousand year tradition
and a tree I cannot heal

Richard S. Parrett

Contributors

Lisa Simpson is a poet from Manchester. She started writing again recently, prompted by a need to find something to focus on in the midst of the pandemic. She had previously been an avid writer as a teenager and had some of her work published at that time. She has most recently had pieces selected for publication by Train River Publishing and has performed at Manchester's Poetry Reverb.

Victoria Punch is a voice coach and musician, writing from her home in Devon between the moors and the sea. She is curious about voice and identity, the limits of language and how we perceive things; her poetry comes from these explorations. More about Victoria can be found on Instagram and Twitter @victoriapunch_ or at www.victoriapunch.co.uk.

Bronwen R. C. Evans is a writer living in Somerset, originally from London. Her main inspirations are found in nature, memory and magic. Bronwen has previously won and followed on to be judge for Folklore Publishing's 'Poems for Trees' competition and is regularly published as part of the editorial board for Hermes magazine. She also has been published by the Blood Moon Poetry Journal, Juno Magazine, Poetic Reveries Magazine and The Teller Magazine. Bronwen has also performed in digital literature festivals and collaborated with the musical group Echoes and Edges.

Samuel Mackereth is a maths teacher and keen outdoors enthusiast who loves nothing more than exploring the muddy fields and woodlands and picturesque hilltops of South Shropshire. Sam writes poetry inspired by nature that explores humanity's relationship with it; he firmly believes that understanding and connecting with the natural world is the best way for us to better understand ourselves and our place as a species. He developed a love of reading and writing poetry as a child but started working on a more cohesive collection during the first Covid 19 lockdown. You can find some of his work on Instagram @english_country_poet.

Barry Hollow lives in Bristol but was born and raised in Ayrshire. He's been published in various publications and journals with his debut collection 'Viaducts and River Views' due for release soon. Barry has been featured regularly on BBC Radio and is emerging on the spoken word scene in Bristol.

Richard S. Parrett moved to the coastal town of Brighton in 2015 and discovered a love of poetry, and in doing so found a more hopeful attitude towards his life and relationships. Richard's writing often includes a physical or emotional journey pieced together by themes of nature and quiet introspection.

Corinna Board lives in a small village in the Cotswolds and works in Oxford, where she teaches English as an additional language. She loves her job, although she often wishes she had more time to write poetry. Her main sources of inspiration are art, nature and mythology. She can be found on Instagram @parole_de_reveuse and on Twitter @CorinnaBoard.

Daniel Moreschi is a poet from Neath, South Wales, UK. After life was turned upside down by his ongoing battle with severe M.E., he rediscovered his passion for poetry that had been dormant since his teenage years. Writing has served as a distraction from his struggles ever since. Daniel has been acclaimed by various poetry competitions, including The Oliver Goldsmith Literature Festival, the Westmoreland Arts & Heritage Festival, the Jurica-Suchy Nature Museum's Nature Poetry Contest, and the Hugo Dock Snow Maze Poetry Contest.

www.blackcatpress.co.uk